A Self-Help Guide

to

Managing Depression

Philip J. Barker

Director of Studies,
Department of Psychiatry,
University of Dundee,
Scotland

CHAPMAN & HALL

London · Glasgow · New York · Tokyo · Melbourne · Madras

Published by Chapman & Hall, 2–6 Boundary Row, London SE1 8HN

Chapman & Hall, 2–6 Boundary Row, London SE1 8HN, UK

Blackie Academic & Professional, Wester Cleddens Road, Bishop-briggs, Glasgow G64 2NZ, UK

Chapman & Hall Inc., 29 West 35th Street, New York NY10001, USA

Chapman & Hall Japan, Thomson Publishing Japan, Hirakawacho Nemoto Building, 6F, 1–7–11 Hirakawa-cho, Chiyoda-ku, Tokyo 102, Japan

Chapman & Hall Australia, Thomas Nelson Australia, 102 Dodds Street, South Melbourne, Victoria 3205, Australia

Chapman & Hall India, R. Seshadri, 32 Second Main Road, CIT East, Madras 600 035, India

Distributed in the USA and Canada by Singular Publishing Group Inc., 4284 41st Street, San Diego, California 92105

First edition 1993

© 1993 Chapman & Hall

Printed in Great Britain by St. Edmundsbury Press, Bury St. Edmunds, Suffolk.

ISBN 0 412 55680 4   1 56593 216 1 (USA)

A catalogue record for this book is available from the British Library

Library of Congress Cataloging-in-Publication data available

♾ Printed on permanent acid-free text paper, manufactured in accordance with the proposed ANSI/NISO Z 39.48–199X and ANSI Z 39.48–1984

understanding your feelings and......
solving your problems

1A   WHAT IS THIS GUIDE ABOUT?

This guide was written to help people who are depressed. At first, you may feel that nothing can be done to help you. Perhaps you want to change things but feel that you do not have the energy. Perhaps you do not know how to.

In the following pages, I shall try to explain what is happening to you. I hope that this will help you understand yourself better. This may be helpful when you try to solve your problems.

In the first section, I offer my view of depression. What might cause depression? What might be done to overcome it? By the time you read this, we shall have begun to work on these questions – to try to solve some of your problems.

1B   OVERCOMING YOUR DEPRESSION

What is depression?

Depression is best understood by looking at its effects. The most obvious sign of depression is a change in your mood. You feel different. You may cry when there is nothing to cry about. You may feel sad and alone in the world. You may lose interest in yourself or others. You may blame yourself for trivial faults or shortcomings. You may even feel guilty about things which happened a long time ago. Sometimes feelings of sadness or emptiness can change dramatically into a false sense of happiness. Sometimes you may get very excited: full of energy and fun. This may only be a mask for the sense of sadness which you feel.

How does depression come about?

These feelings are brought about *mainly* by the way that you think – about yourself, your life and the future. You become depressed because of the way you *interpret* things which happen to you. You may take trivial things too seriously. You may underestimate how well you are coping when things go wrong. You may blame yourself for things which are not your fault.

Although you see your *feelings* as your main problem, in truth the real problem is the way that you think. The way you tend to criticize yourself. The way you try to take responsibility for everything which happens to you. The way you are pessimistic about things ever changing in the future.

Because your 'thinking' is so important, it is worthwhile trying to change how you think. If you can change how you think, this may change how you feel.

Is that all there is to depression?

Thinking plays a large part in making you depressed. Other things are involved too. Things can go wrong with your body. This can make you feel depressed. Some people believe that they become depressed *just* because something goes wrong inside them. This may not be true as far as you are concerned. It may be that *physical* (or bodily) problems, *social* (or life) problems and *psychological* (or thinking) problems have *together* produced your depression.

Some people are more likely to become depressed than others. This has something to do with how their bodies work. This is similar to saying that some people are more likely than others to become overweight or tense or frightened of flying. These also have something to do with physical make-up. But people can *learn* to overcome such problems. In much the same way, you can learn to conquer your depression. It will take a lot of hard work, but it can be done.

What will be involved?

Depression can upset your whole life. The therapy outlined

here aims to help you find out what kind of life problems you have. Then you will learn *how* to solve them. This may ease your distress. It may also help reduce your feelings of depression. The therapy usually goes this way:

First, you learn how to become *more active*. Depressed people often become inactive: they feel that they have no energy, or that activities no longer give them any satisfaction. The first thing you will learn is how to become more active.

The next step helps you to get more *pleasure* and *satisfaction* out of life. Depression often takes this away. You are going to learn how to take it back.

Then you can start looking at the way you think about *yourself*, your *life* and the *future*. You will learn how changing the way you *think* can change the way you *feel*.

Once you know what kind of unhelpful thoughts you are using, you can practise changing the way you think, every day. You learn how to think more constructively about yourself and life in general.

Finally, you will learn how to use this new knowledge to deal better with your life. You will learn how to 'nip problems in the bud'. You will learn how to *avoid* making the mistakes which might bring on another bout of depression.

A word about homework

The therapy is a bit like a college course. Instead of learning about other things, you learn about yourself. Like any course of study, you will have to do some *homework*. Mostly, this will be no more than keeping a note of how you feel from day to day. However, such notes are very important. They show how things change, day by day. Progress sometimes is slow. Every little sign of change is important. Later on you will be able to jot down your thoughts and feelings. These notes will be helpful when you are trying to change the way you think.

From now on, the guidelines are written in the *first person*. I want you to read the rest of this text as if you are talking to yourself. This will help you to *reflect* on your *experience* of depression. This will help you to *consider* other ways of dealing with problems.

1C   ACTIVITY AND DEPRESSION

One of the most obvious signs of depression is that I become less active. Everything seems to be such a chore. Everything seems to be so difficult. Nothing seems to satisfy me. The simplest solution is not to bother.

In this first section, I shall look at the part activity plays in helping me to overcome my depression. I shall look at ways to get myself moving again – especially when I don't feel up to it.

1D   ACTIVITY: A REFRESHER COURSE

Depression is a vicious circle. It slows me down, mentally and physically. One of the first things I may notice is that everything seems such an effort. I get tired easily; I do less than I used to, then I criticize myself for not doing enough. I begin to think I can't do anything at all, and that I'll never get over it. This makes me more depressed. It then becomes even more difficult to do anything. And so it goes on, getting worse and worse.

Stepping out

Activity is one way to break this circle. Becoming more active is important for a number of reasons:

- **Activity makes me feel better.** Activity takes my mind off painful feelings. I begin to feel that I am *taking control* of my life again. I am doing something worthwhile. I may even find that there *are* things that satisfy me, once I try them.
- **Activity makes me feel less tired.** Normally, I rest when I am tired. When I am depressed the tiredness is different. It is a sign that I need to become *more* active – not less. Doing nothing will only make me feel more lethargic and exhausted. Activity will freshen me up: making me *less* tired.
- **Activity makes me want to do more.** Depression often makes me feel like doing nothing at all. When I start becoming active again, the more I do, the more I shall feel like doing.
- **Activity helps me think better.** Once I become more active, I find it easier to solve problems. I start to think more clearly.
- **Activity makes me appear better.** People who matter to me will be pleased to see I am doing more.

Obstacles

Getting going again isn't going to be easy. This is usually because of 'negative thoughts' which stand in my way. These negative thoughts are typical of depression. When I decide to try something, I may find myself thinking:

'I *won't* enjoy it, so why bother?'
'I'll make a mess of it, I *always* do.'
'It's too difficult, I'd *never* manage.'

These *negative* thoughts block me from becoming active. Later on, I will learn to *challenge* these thoughts, to get these obstacles out of my way. For now, I shall simply find out what I am doing, and try to do more of the same.

1E MY LIFE PLAN

People who are depressed often think that they are doing *nothing*. They often think that they are achieving nothing, and enjoying nothing. This is all part and parcel of being depressed. They find it difficult to use their time properly. Often they can't find the time to do things they used to enjoy doing.

I need to start charting what I do. This will show me how I am spending my time. I can use this record to plan my day so that I become more active and my day has a chance of being more enjoyable.

An example

Here is an example which shows what a woman was doing over a whole week. She simply made a note of what she was doing *each hour* of the day. I do not need to write a lot; just make a note. When I discuss my record with my therapist, this will jog my memory. It will remind me of what I was doing at any hour of the day.

	MONDAY	TUESDAY	WEDNESDAY	THURSDAY	FRIDAY	SATURDAY	SUNDAY
8 - 9	had breakfast	—	B/FAST				
9 - 10	Helped with dishes	SAW DOKTOR	WENT TO O.T				
10 - 11	Talked to SARA	UPSET – SPOKE TO B.	O.T.				
11 - 12	—	SLEPT	O.T				
12 - 1	LUNCH	LUNCH	LUNCH – NOT HUNGRY AT ALL.				
1 - 2	TEA + SMOKE	WENT FOR WALK	BUS TO TOWN WITH JANICE				
2 - 3	PHONED J. HAD READ	WENT TO CANTEEN	COFFEE IN LITTLEWOODS				
3 - 4	READING	PHONED DEREK	'WINDOW – SHOPPING'				
4 - 5	TOOK A WALK	WALKING	BACK TO HOSPITAL				
5 - 6	TEA	TEA (NOT HUNGRY)	TEA.				
6 - 7	DID TEA DISHES	DISHES !!	WATCHED T.V. (DOZING)				
7 - 8	WATCHED TV NEWS	READ PAPER					
8 - 9	SLEPT	LAY ON BED					
9 - 10							

Everyday things

For the first few days of this exercise, I shall write down what I am doing *just now*. Just ordinary, everyday things. I don't need to do anything *special*. I shall just practise using the record sheet.

1F MOVING ON

Now I know how I am spending my day. The next step is to plan each day in advance. I am going to plan activities which will give me a sense of satisfaction or enjoyment.

There are three good reasons why I should plan ahead.

1. By planning *in advance*, I shall feel that I am taking control of my life again. It will give me a sense of *purpose*.
2. The plan will prevent me from being swamped by minor decisions. It will keep me going even when I feel bad.
3. When I *write down* my plan, things will look less difficult. I shall have broken down the day into little bits, each of which can be managed on its own. This will be better than trying to fill long, shapeless stretches of time.

Each evening I shall take a few minutes to plan for tomorrow. I shall pick a time when I know I won't be too busy, tired or distracted.

I shall make a note of what I plan to do tomorrow, against each hour of the day. If it's difficult to plan out the whole day, I shall just plan the morning. I can plan the afternoon at mid-day tomorrow.

I shall try to get a balance between activities which might be challenging, but not too difficult, and others which might give me some satisfaction – no matter how little.

I shall remember the golden rule – I WON'T REACH FOR THE STARS. I shall keep my plan simple and not rush myself.

1G FOLLOWING MY OWN DIRECTION

I know how to fill in the plan. Now I shall use it as an aid to overcoming some of my problems. My plan can become a *help* rather than a *hindrance*.

Here are some simple rules for me to follow:

1. **Be flexible**
   I shall use my plan as a *guide,* rather than a god. Of course, things will happen to throw me off my stride. This may make filling in my plan difficult. Someone may ask me to do something or go somewhere. I shall not let this put me off. I shall just carry on filling in the plan when next I can.
2. **Think of other activities**
   Some of my plans will be affected by things outside my control, like the weather or other people's needs. I shall have another activity ready in case my plans are disrupted.
3. **Stick in**
   If I can't do what I had planned, I shall just leave it. I shall not try to do it later on. I shall just carry on to my next planned activity. I shall plan to do what I have missed the *next day.* If I finish something sooner than expected, I shall take a break till my next activity. I can have a cup of tea or read the newspaper. *I shall prepare a menu of such alternatives to choose from.*
4. **Work to the clock**
   I shall try not to be too specific with my plan. I shall avoid being too vague also. 'Tidying up' is too vague. Listing everything I plan to dust is too specific. I need to find a happy medium. 'Read book – 20 minutes' is just right!
5. **Quantity not quality**
   I shall plan to spend *time* (like 30 minutes) on an activity. I *won't* plan how much I *want to achieve* in that time. What I achieve depends on so many other things, like interruptions or things breaking down. If I say that I *must* do all my washing, and for some reason I don't, I shall end up feeling bad. Instead, I shall simply plan to spend some time washing.

   I need to remember the golden rule – IF A THING'S WORTH DOING – IT'S WORTH DOING BADLY.

6. **Stick to the task**

   I need to remember my aim is to stick to my plan. I am *not* planning to overcome all my problems right away. If I work steadily at becoming more active, I shall eventually feel better. I do not expect to get over bad feelings just by watching TV for half an hour.

7. **Retracing my steps**

   At the end of each day, I shall look at what I have done, and what I'd like to change tomorrow. If I did not stick to my plan, I shall not worry. I shall try to find out what was the problem, and how I might change it. Did I plan to do too much? Did I feel tired? Was I aiming for too much success? I can learn from this.

8. **I am always active**

   Sitting in a chair is an activity. So is going to bed, or staring out the window. I am *always doing something*. I need to remember that these activities may not give me much in the way of satisfaction. I need to 'watch' what I am doing: how does it make me feel?

1H   HOW DOES THAT MAKE ME FEEL?

I have been noting what I have been doing from day to day. My next step is to record how I feel about these activities.

From now on I shall record how I feel about what I am doing. I shall find out how much *satisfaction* or *enjoyment* these activities give me.

Activity can give me two kinds of *positive* feelings. I can feel a sense of:

Mastery – when I do something which is difficult, or which I usually avoid doing.

Or I feel a sense of:

Pleasure – when I get some sort of enjoyment from doing something.

I shall measure how much **mastery** or **pleasure** I feel from the things which I am doing each day. There is a simple way of doing this:

1. First of all, I shall write down what I do, hour by hour.
2. Next, I shall try to judge how much *achievement* I got from doing the activity: this is my sense of **mastery**.

I shall measure how much **mastery** I feel, measuring it on a scale between 0 and 10. A score of 0 means that I felt *no sense of achievement* at all. On the other hand, a score of 10 would mean that I felt *a great deal of achievement*.

3. Next, I shall mark this on my plan. I shall put the letter M beside the activity to represent **mastery** and put my score beside the letter. Here is an example below.

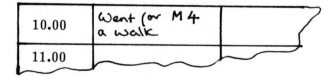

| 10.00 | Went for a walk | M 4 | |
| 11.00 | | | |

4. I shall now try to judge how much *enjoyment* I felt when doing this: this is my sense of **pleasure**.

I shall judge how much **pleasure** I felt, measuring it on a scale between 0 and 10. A score of 0 means I felt *no sense of enjoyment* at all. On the other hand, a score of 10 means that I felt *a great deal of enjoyment*.

5. Now I shall mark this on my plan. I shall put the letter P beside the activity and put my score beside the letter. My example looks like this:

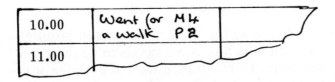

Now my record shows *what I have done*, how much **mastery** I felt, and how much **pleasure** I felt.

I shall *remember* always to record my feelings of **mastery** and **pleasure** *as soon as I have done something*. I *won't* wait until later on. By then I may have forgotten how I actually felt at the time.

Also, I shall try to judge how difficult the activity is for me *now*. I shall try to avoid saying, 'I used to be able to do this with no difficulty'. I shall give myself credit for what I am trying to do *now*.

1I TEN COMMANDMENTS

When I am depressed I often find myself doing the same things every day. I often put off doing the things I *need* to do or would *like* to do. As a result, the pile seems to get bigger and soon overwhelms me completely. How can I start to change this?

There are some things I can do to help myself. I can begin doing what *needs* to be done. I shall:

1. Make a list of all the things I have been putting off.
2. Ask myself which of these needs to be done *first*? Which is next important? Arrange the list in order of priority. If I can't decide, I shall simply put them in alphabetical order. I could stick a pin in the list. The important thing is to do *something*.
3. Take the first task. Break it down into small steps. Ask myself what do I *need to do* to complete it?
4. Go through the steps in my mind: I shall visualize myself doing it. If I think of anything which might stop me doing it, I shall write it down. I shall try to work out how to get round this obstacle. I shall imagine a stream flowing round a rock. How might I 'flow' round this obstacle?
5. Write down any negative thoughts I have about doing things. What do I say to myself which blocks me from doing this?
6. Take each task *step by step*. I shall do it exactly as I did in my mind. I shall deal with any negative thoughts I have by putting them to one side. I shall put them in a box; I shall deal with them later. I shall tell myself just to stick to the task in hand.
7. Stop when I am *winning*. I shall avoid stopping when things start to go badly, as sometimes happens. I shall do just a little bit more – then stop when I am on top. I shall feel so much better.
8. Write down what I have done on my record sheet, as soon as I finish.
9. Focus on what I have *achieved*. I shall avoid thinking about what I still have to do. I shall keep an eye out for

any thoughts which might make my 'success' appear any less than it really is. I shall write these thoughts down also.

10. When I am ready to move on to the next task on my list, I shall acknowledge this – **Well done**.

1J   TEN HELPFUL STICKERS

Here are some hints to help me stick to my plan.

1. **Set aside some time each evening to note what I have done that day, and what I plan to do tomorrow.** I need to choose a time when I won't be interrupted and when I have time to spare.
2. **If I find doing something difficult, I shall tell my body what to do.** I shall give myself specific instructions. Saying 'Go on, do it' or 'Get on with it' is too vague. On the other hand, saying 'Legs, walk' or 'Hand, pick up a pen, hold it, now write' will get me started. I shall visualize myself going through the motions, *seeing* myself doing the activity.
3. **Watch out for unhelpful thoughts.** If I get any unhelpful thoughts I *won't* listen to them – I *shall write them down*. I shall try to answer them, and act on my answers. Once I have dealt with these obstructions, I can tear up the list or set fire to it. (The section on Road Blocks on p202–4 shows me how to do this.)
4. **Get rid of distractions.** Turning off the TV or going off somewhere quiet will help me concentrate upon what I am doing.
5. **Avoid bed.** Bed is for sleeping in, not for *hiding* in during the day. If I need to relax during the day, I shall plan another way of relaxing, like sitting in a comfortable armchair reading, listening to music or taking a bath.
6. **Treat myself for what I have done.** When I have completed an activity I might, for example, plan time for a cigarette or a cup of tea, by way of a treat. These treats are important. They help to spur on and lift my spirits. I shall be good to myself!
7. **Arrange reminders.** I can use a kitchen timer to plan the start and finish of activities. I shall put up signs to remind me what I am supposed to be doing. I shall even *tell* my family or friends what I have planned for a certain time. They can remind me if I get distracted.
8. **Give myself encouragement.** I shall always start the

day with something which will give me a good sense of achievement and which I have a good chance of completing.

9. **Try to balance my day.** I shall aim for a balance between activities which *I need* to do (tasks) and which I used to *enjoy* doing (pleasure).

10. **Do things which I found rewarding or fulfilling in the past.** If I enjoyed things once before, there is a good chance that, once I get going, I shall enjoy them again.

1K   ROAD BLOCKS

When people are depressed, their *unhelpful thinking* keeps them depressed. If depression doesn't just 'pass by', then it is safe to assume that *unhelpful thinking* is keeping me depressed.   •

To overcome my depression I need to 'catch' my unhelpful thoughts as they happen and then *challenge* them. These thoughts are telling me depressing things. That's why I stay depressed. The way to handle these thoughts is to *answer them back*.

Below are some examples of these thoughts. Beside each unhelpful thought is a *suggestion* about how I might answer it back. This is not the *right* answer – or the *only* answer. Just a suggestion. As I practise 'answering back' I shall be able to come up with answers which suit me.

Unhelpful thoughts	Answer
'I can't seem to do anything. It's just too difficult.'	There are problems in doing anything – that's life. How would I deal with this if I wasn't depressed? Is there anyone who can advise me?
' I can't stick to this plan.'	Keeping a plan is a skill. I haven't done this before – doesn't meant that I can't do it if I try. After all, I've used lists before – like for shopping. I could start just by making lists.
'I can't cope any longer.'	I just *think* that because I'm depressed. If I write down what I've got to do, it won't seem so difficult. I don't have to do it all at

Unhelpful thoughts	Answer
	once. I can take one bit at a time.
'It's too difficult.'	It just seems that way because I'm depressed. I've done more difficult things than this before.
'I don't know how to tackle this.'	Have a go – don't try to be perfect. Better to try and see how I get on than not to try at all.
'I don't want to.'	I don't want to do it *now* – but I did earlier on. Anyway, that doesn't matter. The point is, it would be better for me to do it. I *need* to do it.
'I don't think I'm up to it just now. I'll wait till I'm feeling better.'	I won't know if I'm up to it if I don't try. If I wait till I feel like it, I'll never do it. Anyway, doing it will make me feel better.
'There's no point – it'll only make me think of the time I've wasted. I should have done it before.'	I can't waste time. I have just done something else with the time. The point is – what am I doing now? Am I going to repeat myself, or do something different?
'I can't decide.'	The important thing is to do *something*. I could do things in alphabetical order if necessary. Once I get moving, I'll have a clearer idea of where I'm going.

Unhelpful thoughts	Answer
'I'll only make a mess.'	How do I know? I won't know till I try. Anyway, nobody's asking for a star turn. Even if I made a mess of it, it's not the end of the world. I can learn from my mistakes.
'I won't enjoy it.'	How do I know? Since when was I a fortune teller? Try it and see. Be experimental with life.
'I'm not doing anything.'	I shall write down what I do and see if this is right.
'But I'm not doing anything worthwhile.'	Nobody's asking me to judge what I'm doing, *just do it*.
'I don't deserve good things.'	Doing things makes me feel better. That's good in itself. It'll also help me to do things better.
'OK, so I washed the dishes.'	Once, that wouldn't have been very difficult. Now it's very difficult. But in spite of that, I did it. I need to give myself credit for that. My mastery score *should* be 10.

1L WHAT'S THE POINT OF ALL THIS?

Sometimes I may think, 'This is stupid. What's the point in doing all this? This isn't going to make me feel better. What's this got to do with me being depressed?'

Sometimes it is difficult to see how some of these things are going to help. I shall try to overcome this by reminding myself of these 'good reasons' for keeping going.

1. When I am depressed, I often feel that I can do *nothing*. Or I feel that when I do something I *won't enjoy it* or that I *haven't done it well*.

   These records give me a very accurate picture of *what I have done* and exactly *how I felt* about it.

2. Depressed people often tend to see only the black side of things. They see faults very clearly and ignore the good points.

   This is another reason why I should keep these records. If someone asked me tomorrow what I did today, I would probably say: 'Not much' or 'Nothing worth speaking about'.

   This is a natural answer for someone who is depressed: I tend to think in this *negative* fashion. By keeping these records, I can *look back* on what I *actually* did – rather than on what I *think* I did.

These are two very good reasons for keeping these records:

- They give me an honest picture of what I am doing and how I am feeling, during each day; and
- They will be helpful in challenging my *belief* that I do nothing, or that I enjoy nothing.

It is natural to find all of this difficult to do. It may also be hard to understand. I need to remember these points:

- I am trying to find out more about myself – so that I can understand myself and the reasons why I get depressed. The easiest way to do this is by taking 'notes' on what I am doing, and how I react to what I am doing.
- Overcoming depression can be slow at the start. I need to

try not to be too impatient. I need to remember, Rome wasn't built in a day.

- I should remember that much of my present problems stems from my *negative* view of things. I am working towards a more positive view of life and of myself. Even if it doesn't appear to be giving good results, I need to **keep on trying**.

2A I THINK – THEREFORE I AM DEPRESSED

Thinking and depression

Now that I have begun to be more active, I can take a look at my feelings of depression in more detail. What sort of feelings am I getting? What sort of thoughts are related to these feelings?

At the beginning of the guide, I read that my feelings of depression were brought about by the way that I think. In this section, I shall take a close look at the way that I think. What do I think of the things which happen to me? What effect do these thoughts have upon the way I feel?

2B UNHELPFUL THOUGHTS: THE TRUE STORY

Depressed people tend to think in a negative sort of way. They tend to have a negative view of *themselves* ('I'm no good'), their *world* ('Life has no meaning'), and the *future* ('Things will never get any better').

These thoughts make me depressed, and stop me from dealing with my problems. I am now going to look at ways of coping with such thoughts.

Unhelpful thoughts have a lot in common:

1. They are *automatic* – they just 'pop' into my head, without any effort.
2. They are *distorted* – they do not match up to the real facts.
3. They are *very negative* – they keep me depressed and make it difficult for me to change things.
4. They are *plausible* – they appear genuine: I just don't think of challenging them.
5. They are *involuntary* – they are very difficult to switch off.

The more depressed I am, the more unhelpful thoughts I shall have. The more depressed I am, the more I am likely to believe them, and the more depressed they will make me. This is a 'vicious circle'.

Negative thinking has an effect on how I feel and what I do. Now it is time to do something about this.

I shall now take a look at ways of 'catching' my unhelpful thoughts: ways of recognizing *when* I am thinking negatively. Once I can do this, I shall learn how to look for more positive, or helpful, ways of looking at the things which happen to me.

At first, I may find it difficult to 'catch' and answer my unhelpful thoughts. I won't be discouraged. This will get easier with practice. Soon it will become more natural. Catching and answering negative thoughts is a *skill* – something I need to learn. Once I have learned the basics, I shall practise 'catching and answering' my thoughts, as part of my 'homework'.

On the next page is a form which helps me find out what kind of thoughts I have in different situations. It also helps me find out how these thoughts affect the way I feel.

I shall use this form in the first part of this exercise. This will help me become aware of *how* I think.

2C THOUGHT CATCHING

The way I feel is influenced by the way I *think*. I shall practise finding out what sort of thoughts I have when I feel bad. I shall recall the last time I felt bad; I might have felt sad or angry, guilty or frightened. I shall try to remember how I felt and what was happening around me, and answer the following questions.

How did I feel? _____Embarassed_____

How bad was the feeling – measure it by using a scale of 0–100 (100 is the very worst).

_____60_____ **Score**

Situation

Where was I? _In supermarket_

What was I doing? _Shopping – knocked jar off shelf_

What was going on around me? _Assistant stopped to help_

Was I thinking about anything in particular? _How can I pick this up without dropping my basket?_

What thoughts just "popped into my mind" at that time?

Automatic Thoughts		Score
She thinks I'm stupid	100	
Why do I always drop things?	95	
Now I look flustered	90	
I'm just hopeless	80	

Did I *believe* these thoughts? I shall measure to what extent I believed them using a scale 0–100. (0 means I did *not* believe them at all; 100 means I believed them *completely*).

2D HOW YOU THINK

The first step in dealing with my unhelpful thinking is to know *how I think*, and its effect on *how I feel*.

Unhelpful thoughts make me feel bad. They make me feel sad, anxious, hopeless, angry or depressed. Instead of being overwhelmed by these feelings, I can learn to use them as a *signal* for taking some action. I can start taking notice of *when* my mood changes. I can note what was happening and what was running through my mind. If I do this, I shall become more aware of changes in my feelings. I shall also become more aware of the thoughts which spark off these changes in mood. I may find that the same thoughts occur over and over again.

Becoming aware

On the previous page is an example of the form which I can use to practise 'catching' my negative thoughts. This is how I shall use it.

1. Whenever I feel *bad* I shall make a note of 'how I felt', using the scale 0 to 100. The score of 0 means that *I didn't feel bad at all*; 100 means that *I couldn't have felt any worse*.
2. Now I shall make a note of *where I was* when I started to feel bad. Also, I shall write down *what I was doing*, e.g. reading or talking to someone.

   I shall note, also, *what was going on around me*: e.g. people were arguing or the radio was blaring.

   Finally, I shall make a note of any *general thoughts* I was having: I might have been worrying about something or planning a shopping trip.
3. Next, I shall make a note of any *thoughts which 'popped into my head'* just before I started to feel bad. I shall write these down, word for word.

   Some of my thoughts may take the form of 'images'. For instance, I may imagine myself being unable to cope with something or 'going to pieces'. If that happens, I shall just write down what I saw in my mind's eye.

Sometimes I may not be able to identify any thoughts. If that happens, I shall try to imagine what the situation *meant* to me. What does it tell me about myself, my life or the future? This may give me a clue as to why a situation makes me *feel* sad or angry or anxious.

4. Lastly, I shall try to judge how far I *believe* these thoughts. I shall use the same 0 to 100 scale. (0 means that I don't believe them at all, 100 means that I believe them completely.)

Remember, I can score anywhere between 0 and 100.

Take time

It may be difficult to record my thoughts *as they happen*. I won't worry about that. I shall simply make a mental note of the things which have distressed me during the day. Then I shall set aside a few minutes later on to write these down. If I can't remember exactly what happened and what I thought at the time, I shall try doing an 'action replay'. I shall try and remember *what happened*, how I *felt* and what I *thought* at the time.

Take care

I need to beware of 'excuses' for *not* watching my thoughts. I may say 'I'll do it later' or 'I'd better just forget about that'. I may be tempted simply to avoid looking my thoughts in the face. It is quite natural to want to avoid thinking about unpleasant things. I need to remember that, in my case, *confronting* my negative thinking is the best way of fighting my depression.

If I find myself making excuses, it is probably because I have been thinking something really important . . . so I shall *write it down*, I won't hide from it. Once I have done that, I can then practise some distraction to ease my feelings of distress but remember, just ignoring my thoughts won't make them go away.

How many – how often?

Another way of making me more aware of my thoughts is to *count them*. Counting can also make them less distressing. When I count thoughts, this gives me a chance to stand back from myself. It is almost like counting cars which pass me in the street; I would stand to one side in order to count – I would not stand in the middle of the road.

I can count negative thoughts any way that I like. I could tot them up on a knitting counter, or simply tick them off on a card in my pocket or handbag as shown here:

At the end of the day, I can add up how many unhelpful thoughts I have had. I might find myself having more than ever. This is probably just because I am getting better at 'catching' them. In the long run, they will become less frequent.

I need to remember *not* to blame myself for having so many unhelpful thoughts. This is *not* a sign of any weakness or inadequacy on my part.

3A CONFRONTING MY THOUGHTS AND FEELINGS

I have spent some time looking at how I think and how this
affects my feelings. Now I need to look at how I can deal with
these thoughts. In this section, I shall begin to challenge some
of my more common thoughts: thoughts about myself or my
life in general. I shall deal with my feelings by practising
different logical ways of thinking.

In the next few pages, I shall take a look at some general
hints about 'thinking'. I need to acknowledge a simple word
of warning. I have been thinking 'unhelpful thoughts' for a
long time, perhaps for most of my life. I should not expect to
change this pattern easily; the change I desire may take a little
time.

3B CHALLENGING MY DEPRESSING THOUGHTS

Now I am more aware of my depressing thoughts. The next step is to take a closer look at them. Are they really 'true'? Are they really 'helpful'? Is there a more helpful or realistic way of looking at my life?

Questioning my thinking

There are four ways of altering my depressing thoughts. I can ask myself:

1. **What is the evidence?** Why do I think the way I do? What *facts* back up what I think? Do these facts support what I think, or contradict it?
2. **What other views are there?** There is more than one way of looking at a situation. How else could I look at what has happened? I could list other viewpoints. What evidence is there for and against these views? When I look at these objectively, which view appears to be the more correct?
3. **How do these thoughts affect me?** The way I think affects how I feel. How exactly do these thoughts affect how I feel and what I do? How helpful is it to think this way? What are the disadvantages of thinking this way? Can I think of thoughts which might have a better effect upon me?
4. **Am I mistaken?** Depressed people often distort things. They can jump to conclusions; blame themselves for things which are not their fault; exaggerate the importance of things, and so on. Am I making such mistakes about this situation?

Shortly, I shall look more closely at questioning as a way of challenging my negative thinking. Before I do this, I need to look at the record format which will help me do this.

3C A CHALLENGING RECORD

It is important to write down and challenge as many depressing thoughts as I can, each day. When I write them down, I become more objective. Soon I shall be able to challenge such thoughts in my head. At first, it helps simply to write them down. My answers will be stronger if I can read them in black and white. I need to spend some time working out 'challenges' to my thoughts on paper before I can deal with them in my head. The more I practise, the easier it will get.

Over the page is an example of a challenging record. I shall keep this like a daily diary. I shall use it to *confront* my thoughts.

In the first four columns, I shall write down the day and date, how I *felt*, what was *happening* to me, and what I was *thinking*, just as I have done already.

Challenge In the next column I shall write down as many *challenges* to those thoughts as I can imagine. Then I shall ask myself how much I believe these 'other views'. If I don't believe the answer at all, I shall give it a score of 0. If I believe it completely, I shall give it a score of 100. I could score anywhere between 0 and 100.

Outcome In the last column, I need to do three things:

1. Look at my original thought. Now that I have tried to confront it, do I still believe it to the same extent? How far do I believe it now? I shall give it another score out of 100.

   I should find that my belief in the depressing thought has weakened. If it hasn't, perhaps I am ruling out my 'answer' in some way. Maybe I am saying that this may apply to other people, but not to me, or that I am just fooling myself. If I am doing this, I shall write down these new 'depressing thoughts' and try to answer them in the same way.

   I won't expect my belief in the depressing thought to disappear right away. I probably have been thinking such thoughts for some time. The 'answers' which I have come up with are new. It may take some time for me to believe in them completely.

2. Now I shall take a look at my *feelings*. I shall check how I felt before I challenged my negative thoughts. How do my feelings compare now? Do I still feel *exactly* the same? I shall give *each* of the feelings I listed another rating of 100 for severity.

   I should find that my painful feelings have lessened a little. I won't be discouraged if they have not gone away. This will take time and practice. I shall be patient.

3. Lastly, I shall ask what I can *do* to make things better. How might I test out some of the 'helpful answers' I offered as challenges? I need to think about *how I would like to handle that situation* next time it happens. What will I do if I find myself thinking and feeling this way again? I need to work out a plan to stop the same thing happening again. I need to remember to write down exactly what *needs to be done*.

3D A CHALLENGING EXAMPLE

Here is an example of a form which might help me challenge some of the thoughts I commonly use.

CHALLENGING MY DEPRESSIVE THINKING					
DATE	FEELING(S) How do I feel? How bad is it (0–100%)?	SITUATION What was I doing or thinking about at the time?	DEPRESSIVE THOUGHTS What exactly were my thoughts? How far did I believe each of them (1–100%)?	HELPFUL ANSWER What alternatives are there to my depressive thoughts? How far do I believe each of them (0–100%)?	OUTCOME 1. How far do I now believe my depressive thoughts? (0–100%)? 2. How do I feel now (0–100)? 3. What can I do now?
Mon 15th Sept.	Jealous Angry (80)	Got a letter from my sister saying she had just got a new house	How come she has all the luck? My whole life has been a disaster! I'll never get out of the rut (95)	She is lucky to have a new house Everyone can't be so fortunate. I'm not starving am I? I just think my life is a mess (75)	1) Thoughts (50) 2) Feelings (40) 3) I could list my successes. I could save some money. I could list things I'd like to change.

On this illustration, I can see that this person had some bad feelings on Monday 15th September. She received a letter from her sister. She felt angry and jealous. These feelings were about 80% of the *most* she could ever feel. She had *three different thoughts* about this letter. First, 'Why does my sister have all the luck?'. Second, that her 'whole life has been a disaster': and third, that she will 'never get out of the rut'.

At the time, she believed these thoughts about 95%: very strongly indeed.

When she challenged these thoughts, things weren't quite as she thought:

- She said to herself, although her sister was 'lucky to have a new home, everybody can't be so fortunate'.

- She recognized that she just *thought* that her whole life was a mess.
- Finally, she realized that 'never' is a very long time. Perhaps she should try to change her life gradually.

She did not believe these thoughts completely (only about 75%). However, this kind of alternative thinking did reduce her beliefs in her depressing thoughts. After reasoning things out, her feelings of jealousy and anger weren't quite so bad. Finally, she planned to start changing things which she was unhappy about, in a gradual way. Doing what needed to be done!

3E TEN HELPFUL QUESTIONS

Finding 'other viewpoints' can be difficult. Here are ten questions which might help me challenge my negative thoughts.

A. Face the facts?

1. Am I confusing a *thought* with a *fact*? What evidence *supports* these thoughts?
2. Am I ignoring other ways of looking at the situation? What is the evidence *against* these thoughts?

B. Take another look?

3. How do I know my view is the *only* view? How would someone else look at this?
4. Is this just *depressed* thinking? How would I have looked at this before I became depressed?
5. What evidence do I have to support these other ways of thinking?

C. Judge the results

6. Does thinking like this help or hinder me from getting what I want?
7. What are the pros and cons of thinking this way? Would I advise others to think this way – or some other way?
8. Am I asking questions which have no real answers?

D. Try another way

9. Am I overlooking simple solutions? Am I assuming they won't work?

10. How can I test my 'other viewpoints'? What can I do to change my situation?

I shall use these ten questions as an aid to 'challenging' my depressing thoughts.

3F   LOOKING FOR ANSWERS

The ten questions in section 3E will help me find 'other viewpoints'; other ways of thinking about my life. I shall use them as a memory aid. Here are some examples of how these questions can help me think more clearly.

A. Face the facts?

The first thing I need to tackle is the *evidence* for thinking the way I do. Just because I *believe* something to be true does not mean that it *is* true. Would others accept my thought as true? If my thought was put 'on trial', would it stand up in court? Or would it be dismissed as irrelevant or circumstantial?

1. The key question here is, 'Am I confusing a *thought* with a *fact?*'. What is the *evidence* for thinking the way I do? It is not enough to say 'Well, that's what I think!'. What evidence do I have to support this thought?

Automatic thought	Possible answer
(I passed Sally in the street today and she ignored me.) I must have done something to upset her.	Just because she ignored me doesn't mean that I have upset her. Maybe she had something on her mind.

In the example above, the 'depressing (or upsetting) thought' is that someone has hurt me *on purpose*. The assumed 'reason' is that she must be *paying me back* in some way. There is at least one other way of looking at this. Sally may not have seen me, or she might have been thinking about something else.

2. This example shows the need to tell the difference between what I *think* and what is *fact*. The second ques-

tion on my list can help me to look at the situation differently. I need to ask myself, 'What is the evidence *against* these thoughts?'. In the 'possible answer' above, I have done just that.

In challenging my negative thoughts, it may be helpful to remember the idea of the 'court-room battle'. I need to ask myself, 'What is the evidence *for* thinking this way?', then ask myself, 'What is the evidence *against* thinking this way?'.

B. Take another look

The next three questions involve the way I am *looking* at the situation.

3. I need to ask myself if this is the only way of looking at the situation. Often it is difficult to 'step outside myself'. Often it is difficult to be objective. One way to do this might be to ask how someone else (a friend or neighbour) might react to the same situation. How would they look at what has happened? What would they say? If this is still difficult, I could try switching places with my friend. Imagine that what happened to me has happened to a friend. She comes to me for advice or consolation. What would I say to her? *Would I look at the situation differently if it wasn't happening to me?*

Automatic thought	Possible answer
(I went to the shops, I couldn't remember what I wanted.) I'm going off my head!	OK, so I forgot what I wanted. It's hardly the end of the world. My friend Edith is always forgetting things. She just laughs and makes a joke of it.

If my friend said, 'I can't remember things – I'm going off my head', what would I say to her? Would I *agree* with her?

Or would I come up with another way of looking at this problem? Sometimes it is easy to give good advice to our friends; taking my own good advice is often more difficult.

4. In much the same way, our view of things can be another example of depressed thinking. I may *only* be thinking these thoughts because I am depressed. One way to overcome them is to remember how I would have dealt with the situation *before* I became depressed.

Automatic thought	Possible answer
(I picked up a book today. I couldn't concentrate.) This shows how I am getting worse. My mind is deteriorating.	If I wasn't depressed, I'd probably just have moved on to something else. I would probably have said, 'I'll come back to this later, when I feel like reading'.

5. The last question in this section echoes what I have already covered. I need to ask myself what is the evidence *for* thinking in these different ways? Is it *true* that forgetting things isn't the end of the world? Is it *true* that my friend would probably shrug off such a problem? Would I previously have just gone and done something else? If my answer to any of these questions is *yes*, maybe I should swap these thoughts for my negative ones. What would happen if I started to believe in these alternatives?

C. Judge the results

Here are three more questions. These ask how useful are my depressing thoughts.

6. The first question is, 'Does thinking this way help or hinder me from getting what I want?'. Like most people, I simply want to be *happy*. I need to ask myself if thinking

this way helps me to become happy? Or does it stop me from becoming happy? Does this kind of thought make me miserable?

Automatic thought	Possible answer
My life has been a complete mess. I've messed up my own life and now I am messing up everyone else's.	Brooding about what has happened just makes me depressed. What is done is done. I need to put that down to experience. The important thing is to ask myself, 'What am I going to do *now*?'.

Often I feel that I *deserve* to be miserable. Maybe I even feel that I deserve to be *punished* more for things I have done in the past. It is important to challenge these thoughts. These thoughts keep me feeling depressed. Indeed, they may make me feel even more depressed. They also hold me back from getting what I want.

7. In the same vein, I need to consider the pros and cons of thinking in this way. Sometimes depressing thoughts *appear* to be helpful. They may keep me on my toes. But they also have lots of disadvantages. These outweigh any advantages.

Automatic thoughts	Possible answers
'I *must* always try and make a good impression on people.'	Telling myself that I *must* always do anything isn't realistic.
ADVANTAGE = 'I'll go out of my way to be friendly. If they like me in return I'll feel good.'	This just puts more pressure on me. I become more tense and find it even more difficult to relax, concentrate and enjoy myself.
DISADVANTAGE = 'If someone appears not to like me, I'll feel terrible and shall think badly of myself.'	Instead, I shall try thinking, 'If people like me that's nice. If they don't, 'it's not the end of world. It's not realistic to think *everyone* should like me.'

8. Lastly, it may be that I am asking questions which have no real answers. Depressed people often ask themselves, 'Why aren't things different?', 'What is life all about?', 'Why is life so unfair?', 'Why is this happening to me?', or 'What can I do to undo the past?' Brooding over these questions is sure to depress me further. Like it or not, these questions have *no* real answers. I need to try turning these thoughts into a question I *can* answer. If I can't do something, I won't waste any more time on it.

Automatic thought	Possible answer
'When will I get over this depression?'	Sorry! There is no answer to that. Going over and over this just upsets me further. I'd be better asking myself what I can do to make myself *feel* a little better *right now*?

D. Try another way

All of these questions try to change the way I think. They also ask me to do something different as well, like telling myself to stop brooding or to go and do something else for a while.

9. The last two questions ask *how* I can change things. I need to ask, 'Is there a fairly simple solution to my problem? Perhaps one which I have overlooked?' Often, trying to think how a friend, or someone I respect, might handle the situation can help me find such a solution. Or I may know of a 'solution' but have argued that 'It won't do any good. It won't work'. *How will I know unless I try?*

Automatic thought	Possible answer
'I feel awful. I have no energy. I can't stop going over and over things in my mind.'	I know I feel bad. That's what it's like to be depressed. I shall take a short walk in the park. I'll see if a bit of fresh air will refresh me.
'There's no point. Nothing will help me. Anyway, I haven't got the energy.'	Look, I know that I *feel* bad. And I know that I *feel* that nothing is going to change this. But I won't know if this (taking a little walk) is any good until I try it. I shall stop telling myself things won't work. I shall try it and see.

10. In the same way, I shall ask *how* I can *try out* some of these 'possible answers'. I shall start planning *how* I can try 'shrugging things off with a laugh' (instead of worrying if my mind's going). *How* I can deal with my lack of concentration. *How* I can tackle the question of 'What I am going to do with my life now?'.

It is not enough to *think* differently. I need to turn this into **action**. I need to do something different. If I do something different, perhaps I shall *feel* different. *I won't know until I try.*

In the next stage, I shall take another look at the way I think and the effect this has upon my feelings. For the time being, I shall use these ten questions as an aid to challenging my negative thoughts. If I use these questions, I shall begin to bring my depressing thoughts under my control.

A WORD OF CAUTION

Before I leave this section, I should warn myself against expecting too much. There are five problems I might run into when I begin to challenge my negative thoughts.

1. Firstly, 'confronting thoughts' is unusual. Normally we don't stand back, question and 'challenge' our thoughts. What I am asking myself to do is difficult. At first I may find it near impossible to be objective. I may find that my 'answers' do not appear to affect my feelings very much. **I shall not despair**. This is quite normal. I need to give myself the chance to practise this challenging approach. I need to give myself time to get the hang of it. I won't be discouraged if I can't master it straight away. After all, I wouldn't expect to be able to drive after only a few lessons. *Practice, practice* and more *practice*.

2. I may also find it difficult to come up with alternatives when I am feeling upset. The feelings may be so bad that I may think that I cannot think at all. If this happens, I shall write down what is distressing me as a *distraction*. When I feel calmer, I shall come back to notes. Now I shall be in a better position to look for more helpful answers.

   I need to beware of making matters worse by telling myself that this means that I am a failure, or that this isn't working.

3. I need to remember that my record is just a record. It does not have to be good, well-written, or anything special. I am using it to confront my thoughts and feelings. It is not using me! There are no 'right' or 'wrong' answers – I am working out what will change things *for me*! What will weaken my faith in these depressing thoughts?

4. I need to beware of criticizing myself when I am writing down my thoughts. I might find myself thinking, 'I must be stupid to think that' or 'This just shows how bad I really am'. I need to *remember* that these are more examples of depressing thoughts. This is part and parcel of my depression. My negative thinking is the problem: not my intelligence or my goodness. I am good just because *I am*.

5. Lastly, I shall not get upset if I find the same thoughts cropping up over and over again. My depressing thinking is well established. My thinking has become a bad habit which will take some time to break, like giving up smoking or trying to stop biting my nails. I shall take the view that the more often a particular thought occurs, the more chances I have to challenge it, and break the habit.

4A   UNHELPFUL THOUGHTS

I have been introduced to the idea of unhelpful thoughts and the part they play in negative thinking. In this section, I shall focus upon these unhelpful thoughts in more detail. Here, I shall develop my awareness of the kind of unhelpful thoughts *I* make, as I make them.

If I can learn to 'catch' my unhelpful thoughts, I may be able to prevent patterns of unhelpful thinking becoming established.

CLEAR, COOL THINKING

Over the next few pages are some of the common unhelpful thoughts which trouble depressed people. It is worth noting that they trouble *most* people, but they trouble depressed people more seriously. These are examples of *unhelpful* thinking. When I use them I say something to myself which is not true, is an exaggeration of the truth, or is not supported by any evidence. These ways of thinking put me down in some way. They make me feel bad. They are very unhelpful. I intend to study these so that I can recognize them better. It's like the old saying: 'To be forewarned is to be forearmed'. If I can catch these ways of thinking early on, I may be able to confront them more quickly. As a result, I may be able to avoid feeling distressed, or I may be able to reduce the extent of any bad feelings.

I shouldn't be surprised if I find that I don't use all of these thoughts. I may use some more often than others. I may not be aware of some of these at all. However, it is only to be expected that I shall use some of them quite often. These are the real culprits as far as my depression is concerned.

These unhelpful thoughts have been illustrated with little pictures and symbols. I shall make a copy of these to keep in my pocket or handbag to help me recognize the unhelpful thoughts, and to challenge them.

At this stage, I am learning how to recognize these unhelpful thoughts so that I can catch them all the more easily. Now I am becoming more knowledgeable about what *influences* my feelings of depression, I am becoming more able to catch the unhelpful thoughts which influence my feelings of depression.

EMOTIONAL REASONING

Human beings tend to be emotional. Our hearts rule our heads much of the time. However, I need to watch that such 'emotional reasoning' doesn't lead me into trouble. Do I ever think, 'I feel guilty. This must mean I've done something wrong.' Or, 'I know that I can't prove it but I just *feel* that it's true.' These are both examples of *emotional reasoning*: letting my heart rule my head.

Again, it is important that I search for the evidence to support feeling this way. If I can't find any, I shall have to try to accept that I am being 'emotional'. I am putting myself down for no good reason. I have a choice. I can continue to 'feel' guilty or let down (or whatever) for no good reason, or I can say there is no reason *why* I should feel this way. Then I can try to work out how I should be feeling and what I should do next!

Do I ever say, 'I *should* be able to pull myself together', or, 'I *must* always try to appear cheerful', or, 'I *should* always want to be with my family'? These kind of thoughts make heavy demands upon my emotions. They make me feel I am a failure (if I am not always cheerful); or they make me feel guilty (if I don't always want to be with my family).

SHOULDS + MUSTS

It is one thing to try to be positive, cheerful or loving. It is quite another to say that I *should* or *must always* be like that. When I find myself using 'should and must', I shall simply tell myself to *stop trying to be perfect*. I can go ahead and try to be positive or loving or cheerful. But I won't punish myself if I can't always keep it up.

JUMPING TO CONCLUSIONS

Often, I may tell myself that things are 'bad', although I have no evidence to support this. This is a bit like crystal-ball gazing. I am predicting that certain things *will* happen – a bit like a fortune teller. I may tell myself that, 'I'll never get over this' or, 'I'll never be able to do that'. How do I know? Can I foretell the future? At other times, I may say that, 'Everyone is fed up with me' or, 'People don't like me any more'. How do I know? Can I read their minds? Jumping to conclusions is a very common error – all people tend to do this from time to time. The easiest way to challenge this error is to look for the evidence. How do I *know* that this or that will happen? How do I *know* that people don't like me or don't want me? There is no point just saying, 'Well, I feel that way'. This is a sign that I am *jumping to conclusions*.

Lots of people tend to exaggerate. Maybe I do this as well. If something goes wrong, do I ever say, 'Oh, this is terrible, and there's nothing I can do about it'? I may well be *magnifying* the problem – almost as though I was holding a magnifying glass over it. I make it look worse than it really is. At the same

CATASTROPHIZING

time, I can *underestimate* my ability to deal with things – almost as if I was looking at my own abilities down the wrong end of a telescope.

I make them appear much *smaller* than they really are. I minimize myself – I make myself appear less able or less competent.

When things go wrong, I shall try to avoid turning a small problem into a disaster or a complete 'catastrophe'. I shall search for the evidence. How bad is it *really*? Is it really so terrible? Is it really the worst thing which could happen to me? Am I really not able to do anything? I shall make a list of the sort of things I might at least try.

MENTAL FILTER

Most things which happen to me will not be all bad. They will be made up of 'bad bits' and 'good bits'. Do I tend to think only of the bad bits? This is a bit like making coffee with ground coffee. However, instead of keeping the water which passes through the ground beans, I keep the grounds instead. Even when making coffee, there is a 'good bit' (the coffee liquid) and a 'bad bit' (the coffee grounds). When I find myself saying, 'I didn't have a minute's happiness today' or 'My life has been just one problem after another', I may well be using the *mental filter*. I may be concentrating only upon the bad bits – throwing away any 'good bits'. I can start tackling this error by checking the evidence. I can make a list of all the 'bad bits' and then try to list the 'good bits' – no matter how small they appear by comparison. I need to beware of 'filtering' out the bad experiences, and then focusing all my attention upon them.

DISCOUNTING THE POSITIVE

In a similar way, I might be telling myself that some 'good bits' *don't count* for some reason. I might say, 'OK, so I did some work today. So what? I do that every day. It's hardly a success'. I may be telling myself that certain things don't count as positive experiences. I reject these and end up dwelling upon negative experiences (the 'bad bits'). This error is another version of the mental filter. If I am obliged to recognize something which isn't really *bad*, I discount it by saying that it's not really good either. It's nothing. I need to remind myself that filtering out good experiences only worsens my depression. *Discounting the positive* is another way of focusing on bad experiences and another way of deepening my depression.

Do I tend to see things in 'black and white'? For instance, am I either a *total* success or a *total* failure? If *one* thing goes wrong, does this mean that *everything* is wrong? This error can be called 'all-or-nothing thinking.' I seem to be saying to myself, 'If I am not perfect, I must be a complete mess', or, 'If everyone doesn't love me, then nobody loves me'. I am making it a case of *all or nothing*.

BLACK + WHITE THINKING

I need to check this error by asking myself, 'What is the evidence for saying that *everything* is wrong, or that *nothing* is right?'. It may be true that *some* things are wrong, or that *some* improvement could be made in a situation. This is not the same as saying that everything is wrong, or nothing is right. I need to remember that reality is made up of a thousand shades of grey. I am not all good or all bad, all right or all wrong. *There is no black and white.*

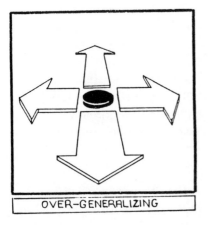

OVER–GENERALIZING

Do I tend to use one bad experience to colour other parts of my life? Do I ever make a mistake, or fail at something and say to myself, 'I never get *anything* right'.? This is an example of *over-generalization*. Just because I fail at *one* thing doesn't mean that I shall fail at *everything*. Maybe I fall out with a friend and end up saying, 'Nobody loves me'. I am taking my feelings from one situation and colouring other situations in an equally bad way.

The best way to tackle this is, once again, to ask for the evidence. How do I know that nobody loves me or that I never get anything right? There is no need to pretend that there is *no* problem. But there is no value in transferring my unhappiness from one situation to the rest of my life. I need to tell the difference between things which are really 'bad' or unpleasant and those which I have 'coloured' black, by over-generalizing.

LABELLING

When things go wrong, I may find myself sticking labels on myself. When I have a quarrel with someone, this may *mean* that I am a 'rotten person'. When I try to tackle something but give up, this *means* that I am 'hopeless' or 'useless'. I find it difficult to recognize that I am made up of 'good bits' and 'bad bits' – like other people. The label I apply usually suggests that I am *completely* bad, hopeless or useless.

To check this error, I need to ask for the evidence. How do I know that I am *completely* bad? How do I know that I shall not succeed next time round? How do I know that other people wouldn't have found this equally difficult? I need to beware of *labels* – they usually hide the truth.

The last error involves thinking that 'Everything always happens to me.' I may think that bad things – like a sudden downpour on a sunny day – only affect me. This is just another example of my bad luck, or I may think that in some way it is my fault. If people have an argument, it may be as a result of something *I* have said. Or, if someone is unhappy, it is

PERSONALIZATION

because I must have upset them. Although it is difficult to accept, the truth is that I am not really that important. Nobody is *that* important. Unless I can *prove* to myself that it is my fault – by pointing to some evidence – I shall have to accept that I am making the error of *personalization*. I am tricking myself into thinking that things always happen to me, or are my fault. This simply is not true.

5A PUTTING MY THOUGHTS TO THE TEST

I have now learned to 'catch' my negative thoughts. I have some practice in arguing them into submission. I have learned a bit about replacing depressing thoughts with more reasonable 'answers'.

I have begun to use these 'possible answers' to change the way I act. In this section, I shall go a stage further. Now I shall learn how to become my own 'problem solver'. I shall learn how to put my depressing thoughts to the test. Now is the time to start experimenting with my life. Through these experiments, I can find the real value of my 'possible answers'.

5B ACTION STATIONS

In the last two sections, I focused on arguments *against* my negative thoughts. Changing the way I think can do wonders for the way I feel. Just arguing with myself is, however, not enough. I can tell myself that these depressing thoughts are unhelpful, *but do I really believe it*? I really need to test out some of my 'possible answers'. I need to take some of my own advice, by changing the way that I act. In this section, I shall look at this in more depth. I shall consider how I can *challenge* my depressing thoughts further, by *discovering* how wrong they are.

I have already considered some ways of 'collecting evidence' which contradicts my negative thoughts. Now it's time to *act* on my 'possible answers'. Action will help me to break my old thinking habits. It will also help me to strengthen my new (more positive) ways of thinking.

Testing! Testing!

I may not think it, but I am a bit of a scientist. I make predictions about my world. Then I act on these predictions. For instance, I might predict that, 'If I press this bell, some-one will come to the door'. I might predict that, 'If I stood in the pouring rain, I would not only get wet but would also catch cold'. When it comes to dealing with people, I might predict that, 'If I argue with my husband, he will stop loving me'. The important thing about such predictions is that I act on them *automatically*. Very rarely do I ask if my predictions are true or not. *I do not test out my predictions*.

A person who is depressed is a bit like a scientist gone wrong. Instead of finding out if her predictions are true or not, she distorts her view of the world to fit her prediction.

Most of the depressing thoughts I have considered involve prediction. I might tell myself that, 'I shall *never* get over this', or, 'People *won't* like me', or, 'If I do that, people *will* be upset'. In the last two sections, I have been trying to develop the idea of thinking like a 'personal scientist'. I have been *helping* myself *question* my depressing thoughts. Instead of accepting these thoughts, now I am looking for alternatives.

Taking action

Six steps are needed to *test* my predictions. I need to:

1. Think of my prediction (or depressing thought).
2. Ask what is the evidence *for* and *against* thinking this way.
3. Think of how I can test out my prediction. This will be a small-scale *experiment*.
4. Try out my experiment.
5. Make a note of what happens *as a result*.

   - If my prediction is shown to be false, so much the better. I have reason to believe my 'possible answers' even more strongly now.
   - If my prediction is shown to be true, *I need not worry*. This is still useful. I now have a chance to see where I was going wrong. I can work out how to think *differently*. Once I have worked out an alternative, I can test this again, in another *experiment*.

6. Draw some conclusions. I have learned something from my experiment. What *exactly* have I learned? I need to make a careful note of this, for future reference.

Here are a couple of examples to illustrate the process of being a 'personal scientist'.

Harriet

Harriet finds it difficult to talk to the other women on the ward. She thinks that she doesn't have anything to say. She regrets her lack of education. For this reason, she usually avoids mixing with the other women.

1. **Prediction** If I talk to people, they will find out how stupid I am. They will laugh at me and I will get upset.

2. **The evidence** I only *think* that they are smarter than me. Anyway, there are lots of things I am interested in which I could talk about. Other people say 'stupid things' and laugh *along* with everyone else. How do I know that people aren't laughing just because they are happy? Anyway, what's so bad about having a poor education? There are more important things about a person than whether or not she can talk clever, like being honest, or loyal or friendly.
3. **The plan** I shall listen and say *one* thing, anything, and see what happens.
4. **The test** How do I know I *shall* get upset if I don't try? I shall sit in on the group. I'll just listen at first and talk when anyone speaks to me. I'll try and relax and show an interest in what's being said. I need to remember to smile at people. Look interested and other people might like it.
5. **The result** It was easier than I thought. By listening to everyone else, I was less self-conscious. I said something and everyone laughed. At first I blushed and was about to worry but I checked myself. 'See', I said, 'I've cheered somebody up.'
6. **What I learned** My prediction was quite wrong. I won't say it was easy, but it wasn't half as bad as my depressing thoughts said it would be.

Mary

Mary is depressed. She can't seem to do anything to shift it. She tries reading but can't concentrate. She tries to watch television but her mind wanders on to 'negative depressing thoughts' again. She despairs of ever getting better.

1. **Prediction** I am never going to get any better. My mind is going. I can't do anything at all. I'm going to get worse. I know I am.
2. **The evidence** I know I *feel* that I'm never going to get better. But that's just depressive thinking. My mind isn't really going. This difficulty in concentrating is all part of depression. Maybe I'm trying too hard. And there are

some things that I do. However, I only think about things I find difficult.

3. **The plan** I'll tackle something *small* and see what happens.
4. **The test** I shall try reading just a little bit – maybe just a page. Just to see if I can do it. Then I'll try watching a short TV programme, like the news.
5. **The result** Well, I read the page. But what's a page? Wait a minute, that's another depressing thought. Putting myself down again. Yes, I said I would try a page and I did that. *Good*. Watching TV was more of a problem. The room was a bit noisy. I found it difficult to concentrate. But I kept my attention on the TV at least. *Good*. Someone said, 'Aren't you waiting for the next programme?' and I just said, 'No, I've got something to do'.
6. **What I learned** I found out that my predictions were quite wrong. I *can* do things as long as they are realistic. Rome wasn't built in a day. I need to take things in smaller steps. And I need to give myself more encouragement.

This is a very important stage for me. Although challenging my depressing thoughts is important, putting them to the test is *the big step*. At the start of this guide, I found out that my problems stemmed from how I think about things which happen to me. Here, I have thought about putting my negative thoughts to the test. Are these thoughts really *true*? Or am I *talking myself into believing they are* – without any evidence?

Sometimes things will happen which will be unpleasant. I can use these experiences to learn that life is not always pleasant. Often it can be very unpleasant. I need to be able to tell the difference between things which *are* unpleasant and things which *I think* are unpleasant. Often there is not much I can do about *really* unpleasant things. But there is a lot I can do to change my negative thoughts. Those which make me *feel* unpleasant. Putting my thoughts and predictions to the *test* is an important part of this change.

6A SETBACKS

I am at the stage where I am dealing directly with the thoughts which made me feel depressed. I have learned a lot about the kind of unhelpful thoughts I can make and how to challenge them. Will it now all be plain sailing? Probably not. The road to recovery is likely to be strewn with all sorts of obstacles. Some will stop me in my tracks. These obstacles might knock me back a bit. They might be distressing. **I won't despair**. Such setbacks are only to be expected. They are all part of my stages of recovery.

In the next few pages, I shall think about ways of handling these setbacks. Here I can learn how to deal with setbacks when they have happened. I can also learn how to try to ensure they don't get any worse.

6B BOUNCING BACK

Getting over depression means making changes in my life. When making such changes things rarely go smoothly all the time. At times things go well. I think that I am almost over my problems. Then I hit some 'black spots'. I think that my depression is overtaking me again. Things start to go wrong. Maybe *everything* seems to be going wrong. I wonder if things will ever get better. I may even wonder if there is any point in going on. Perhaps something has upset me. Or I may just wake up one day, feeling like this.

One thing needs to be said about this. **It is absolutely okay to have days like this!** This is just another stage on the road to recovery. They are not a sign that I shall never overcome my depression. Although unpleasant, setbacks have a good side. Setbacks let me learn more about myself. They give me a chance to practise the skills which I have learned about dealing with depression. Maybe I should go as far as trying to make myself depressed. By doing this *consciously*, I learn that I can push myself down into a deep depression. Once I have done that, I can pull myself out again, *by my own efforts*. Getting over setbacks is the stage where I learn to build up my confidence. Confidence in *my* ability to control *my* depression. This is the ownership of *me*!

Here are some basic rules about dealing with these setbacks. First, I shall consider how to deal with a setback when it catches me unawares. Then, I shall consider how to develop my own plan for dealing with problems in the future.

6C SOME BASIC RULES

Avoid the panic button

Getting caught by a setback can be upsetting. I need to remember that they are an acceptable part of getting over depression. Even people who are not depressed have their 'ups and downs'. When I am depressed, however, the downs seem to go deeper. They seem more difficult to climb out of. This is only how it *seems*. I need to tell myself very firmly – *'No need to panic'*.

Use what I have learned

People often take a setback to mean that they are 'back to square one'. They often take this as meaning that they have failed. I need to ask myself, 'Have I been able to work things out in the past? What evidence have I to show this? Does this not mean that I can use these skills again, this time round?' I need to try out what I know. I need to stick with these new skills. What have I got to lose?

Change the frame

I shall look on setbacks as being useful. I shall try to put them in a new context. Instead of being scared, I shall look on this as a challenge. This is giving me a chance to show my stuff! By changing the 'frame', I am turning a problem into an opportunity. I am getting a chance to learn more about myself.

Go back to basics

By the time I read this, I shall have made some progress. I may be at the stage of challenging depressing thoughts as they crop up. I have worked through several 'stages' of the therapy. That doesn't mean that I can't go back to using some of the more basic methods to control my feelings. Maybe I find it difficult to answer certain negative thoughts. This may make me feel 'down'. I need to get myself moving again by *going back to basics*. I need to use distraction: steer my thoughts away from my painful feelings. I need to start using my life plan again. I need to plan for tomorrow. I need to use the M and P rating to help me 'rediscover' some of my satisfying activities.

Why don't I try writing down my thoughts again? If something is proving difficult to do, why don't I *write down* what it is I have to do; I could break it down into stages, the way I used to do. Even people who have never been depressed find this a useful way of dealing with difficult problems. I need not be embarrassed that I have to go back to basics. It's the easiest way to get going again. It makes sense.

Watch my black and white

As I make progress, the worse my 'down' spell will seem by comparison. In a strange way, my 'setback' is a sign of progress. I am upset by the fact that I have 'slid back' or I am 'running into difficulties'. I only think this because I have *something better* to compare my depression with. I need to remember that 'ups and downs' are part of everyday living. I need not let my 'black and white thinking' add to my depression.

Add up my gains

When I fall into depression again, it often seems as though everything is lost. **This is not true**. Nothing can take away the gains which I have made. Even if they seem to have gone now, they will come back as my depression lifts again. I can help to speed this up by remembering all the things I learned to do, or picked up again recently. Why don't I write them all down? Make a list of all the challenges I faced, no matter how small. There is no need to stint myself. Why don't I add up each and every gain I have made recently?

Don't blame myself

One of the easiest mistakes to make when I am feeling depressed is to blame myself for what has happened. Is blaming myself going to help? Earlier I found out that setbacks are just a part of recovery from depression. Instead of heaping blame on to myself, why not look upon it as a problem to be solved, another challenge? I won't use my setback as a stick to beat myself with.

Let's hang on!

If I don't seem to be able to solve the problem, I don't need to despair. I don't need to give up. Time and a little sustained effort on my part is what is needed. I need to remember the times in the past when I thought that all was lost. Things looked black then, didn't they? But I got over it. This time will be no different. I can bring myself through. I just need to remember, when the going gets really tough, it's time for me to get tougher. **Hang on in there!**

Confronting setbacks

A good way of learning to handle setbacks is to develop my own plan for what to do when one happens.

To help me do this, I shall sketch out *two* plans:

Plan A tells how I can make myself as *miserable* as possible. This can be used to keep me miserable for a long time. The idea behind this plan is to help me become aware of how I act or think in ways which make me depressed. The sooner I know what I am doing, the sooner I can do something to change it.

Plan B is just the opposite. This plan shows me how I can take steps to overcome my depressive thinking. This plan helps me to work out ways of challenging these thoughts, and changing the way I feel.

On the next page are examples of these plans. Each plan is made up of thoughts and actions. Things I could say to myself, and things to do. These are not the *only* thoughts and actions which I could use. They are just examples of what I might try. I might want to work out some plans of my own, based on my own experiences. I could ask myself what sort of things I have thought about or done in the past which have made me feel more depressed? What sort of thoughts or actions have I used which have made me feel less distressed, or even a little better?

Example

Plan A	Plan B
Stay in bed.	Get up and get busy. I know from experience that it will be an effort to start with, but it will get easier as I go along, and I will feel better for it. Hiding in bed won't help at all.
Spend as much time as possible brooding and feeling miserable.	Involve myself in something. Use distraction techniques. Do something active that needs a bit of concentration. I shall come back to answering thoughts later, when I feel better.
Leave the day shapeless and vague, and tell myself it's all too much for me.	Plan, in detail, exactly what I am going to do. Record what I do, and give myself marks for **mastery** and **pleasure**.
Don't do anything I enjoy. Tell myself I don't deserve it.	Make a point of doing things I enjoy, and noticing small pleasures. It will help me to get out of the depression and I will end up doing the things I have to do more efficiently.

Example

Plan A	Plan B
Don't give myself any credit for anything.	Acknowledge *everything* I achieve. Remind myself that when I am feeling really bad, even the simplest activity is an achievement. If I can, I shall try and do one extra thing beyond my normal routine. It will make all the difference to the way I feel.
Tell myself that I am weak and pathetic for being this way.	Remind myself that self-criticism does nothing to help me overcome my depression – in fact, it will make me feel worse. Give what is happening its proper name – it is a *setback*. It is nothing to do with me being weak or pathetic. I need to remind myself that it is OK to have setbacks. I need to try to see this one as a problem I can tackle. It is not a reflection of my inadequacy as a person.
Tell myself I should be over my depression by now.	Remind myself that there is no *should* about it. I need to think of all the things I have been doing to overcome this very tough problem and allow myself credit for what I have achieved.

Example

Plan A	Plan B
Think about all the things I have done wrong in my life. Blame myself for them and tell myself what a horrible person I am.	I need to tell myself that I am only human. Of course I have made mistakes in my life – who hasn't? I need to remember that I wouldn't expect that kind of perfection of anyone else. I need to ask myself if, in fact, a lot of the things I have done wrong were done in good faith – they seemed the best possible alternative at the time. I need to remember that I've done millions of things in my life, good, bad and indifferent. It is not fair to judge myself only on the basis of the bad ones. I need to think about some of the good things I have done instead.
Tell myself this approach is not going to work. I might as well give up. I'll always be this way.	I need to remind myself of what I have already achieved with it. If this has worked before, it will work again, even though it may be difficult to get started. A setback does not mean all is lost – it's a passing phase, and I can learn from it. I must remember the times when this has happened in the past.

WHAT DO I BELIEVE, ANYWAY?

Different people see the world in different ways. Some people are optimists, others are pessimists. Some people are philosophical about life – others see disaster at every corner. How people judge things which happen to them in their lives depends upon their beliefs and attitudes. What things do they value? What do they consider important?

What are my basic values, beliefs or attitudes? The thoughts I have about my world and myself are based upon these. I assume that certain things are important – why else should I get concerned about them? I value some people and certain things very much – that is why I get upset at the thought of losing them. I believe that certain things are necessary for me to lead a satisfactory life – this is why I so often say this 'must' happen or that 'should' have happened.

These ideas help me to judge my own personal worth – they tell me if I am doing OK or not. I have already discovered how holding very negative thoughts about myself, or things that happen, can be very unhelpful. Is the same true of extreme beliefs? If I believe that certain things must be the case, will that belief be my undoing?

Discovering my values

How can I go about finding out what my beliefs are? One way would be to ask myself what situations mean – or what they say about me. If I am upset over something, for example falling out with a friend, I might ask myself: 'What is so bad about falling out with someone? In what way is that a problem for me?'

If I tell myself it is because she won't like me any more, what does that mean to me: 'What is so bad about someone not liking me any more?'.

I might end up telling myself that I can't live without friends, or that it would be just awful if something like that happened. This might be an example of one of my extreme beliefs, that: 'I cannot be happy unless people care about me'.

Using a checklist

Alternatively, I could use a checklist or questionnaire to find out what my beliefs are. I could ask myself, do I need:

- approval from other people? Do I get angry or depressed when people do not show that they approve of me?
- love from others? Do I tend to try not to upset my friends or partner for fear that they might stop loving me?
- success to prove my self-worth? Do I get depressed when I fail at things, or things don't go the way I planned?
- to be perfect? Do I get upset over making mistakes or little failures? Am I always pushing myself to chase goals which may be unrealistic?
- to get things by right? Do I get angry or upset if I don't get the things I want? Do I get upset if I fail to get recognition for what I have done?
- to be the centre of my world? Do I tend to blame myself for everything that happens? Do I feel guilty because I cannot influence my family or friends, or feel threatened when they disagree with me?
- to be dependent? Do I tend to rely on other people, luck or good fortune to bring happiness or meaning to my life? Do I get upset when I appear to be unlucky or I am not supported by a supply of 'good things'?

Dealing with unhelpful beliefs

I need to question whether or not any of these beliefs help me to live a satisfactory life. Do they, perhaps, make my life more difficult by setting impossible demands? I need to challenge these beliefs in the same way as I confronted my depressing thoughts. I need to find alternatives which will help me to do what I need, and want to do, in my life.

Because of their hidden nature, it is difficult to unearth beliefs and attitudes. I need to commit myself to studying my beliefs over a long period of time. I shall not expect to find out all about myself in a few days or even weeks. I need to continue keeping a watching brief on all my depressing thoughts, asking myself from what extreme beliefs they might have come. In time, it may become clear to me where these ideas about life came from. Then I might be able to cast them off in favour of some new, more helpful beliefs about life and myself. Till then, I shall keep on watching, confronting and finding alternatives.

REFERENCES

Beck, A.T. and Greenberg, R.L. (1974) *Coping with Depression*. New York, Institute for Rational Living, Inc.

Gunning, R. (1952) *The Technique of Clear Writing*. New York, McGraw-Hill.